THE ADVEN[illegible] OF A BEAR CALLED PADDINGTON

Adapted by
ALFRED BRADLEY
from the stories by
MICHAEL BOND

SAMUEL

FRENCH

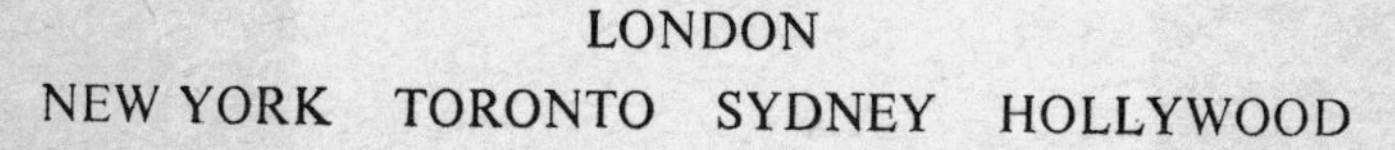

LONDON
NEW YORK TORONTO SYDNEY HOLLYWOOD

ISBN 0 573 05035 X

Please note our NEW ADDRESS:

Samuel French Ltd
52 Fitzroy Street London W1P 6JR
Tel: 01 - 387 9373

PADDINGTON BEAR

Although Paddington's adventures make up a full-length play lasting about two hours, each episode is a complete story in itself and may be performed as a one-act play. Alternatively it is possible to link several episodes together omitting those which require more elaborate technical resources. Each adventure is introduced by a short scene at the Browns' house to give time for the next setting to be moved into position.

A percussionist equipped with a wide range of accessories will emphasize falls and bumps, point Paddington's "stare", help to bridge the scenes and generally add to the excitement.

Paddington's costume is important. Many children will have a clear idea of his appearance before the play begins and producers should be guided by the Peggy Fortnum illustrations in the Paddington books. A character make-up chosen to blend with the fur hood of the costume is preferable to a mask which tends to muffle the voice and permits the actor only a very limited range of expression.

There are a number of points in the script where the characters ask themselves questions and it is important, particularly at the beginning, to allow time for the audience to supply the answers so that they realise that they may join in. If the convention is established early, the audience will give warnings, advice and encouragement without having to be *asked* to participate.

THE ADVENTURES OF A BEAR CALLED PADDINGTON

CAST

Henry Brown
Mary Brown, his wife
Judy, their daughter
Jonathan, their son
Mrs Bird, their housekeeper
Mr Gruber, a friendly shopkeeper
Mr Curry, a peppery neighbour
Paddington

and:
Bert, a station porter
Fred, a man with a refreshment trolley
Miss Block, a member of the Arts Society
Mervyn Scrape, R.A., the Arts Society judge
Flo, who looks after the launderette
Nurse Kay
Police Constable
Flash Harry, a photographer
Sir Archibald, a surgeon

The smaller parts may be doubled by two men and two women.

MUSIC
Bert Chappell

LYRICS
Bert Chappell, Brenda Johnson, Alfred Bradley

Copies of the music may be obtained from:
SOUTHERN MUSIC PUBLISHING COMPANY LTD.
8 DENMARK STREET
LONDON WC2 8LT

And also from:
SAMUEL FRENCH LTD

ACT I

A frontcloth of part of Paddington Station with the name prominent. Paddington is sitting on a platform trolley concealed behind assorted mail bags, parcels and luggage. Henry Brown comes on to the platform closely followed by his wife. At some time during the following, a portly gentleman enters the stage

Mr Brown Well, Mary, after all that rushing about, we're here early.
Mrs Brown What's the time now?
Mr Brown It's only a quarter past four and Judy's train doesn't arrive until half past.
Mrs Brown Are you sure?
Mr Brown I checked up this morning.
Mrs Brown I'll just go and see which platform it's due in on.

Mrs Brown exits

Left to himself Mr Brown strolls around the platform trolley. As he taps his pipe on the handle, a furry bundle hidden behind the parcels pops up like a jack-in-the-box and quickly down again. Mr Brown starts back then returns to the trolley. He pokes the furry object gently, it stirs and subsides again.

Mrs Brown returns

Mrs Brown It's platform five. And you're quite right, the train doesn't arrive until half past four.
Mr Brown Mary, I've just seen something extraordinary.
Mrs Brown Oh? What's that?
Mr Brown Er . . . well, it's a bear.
Mrs Brown A bear? On Paddington Station. Don't be silly, Henry. There can't be.
Mr Brown But there is. I distinctly saw it. Over there . . . behind the trolley. It was wearing a funny kind of hat. Come and see for yourself.
Mrs Brown (*humouring him*) Very well, dear. (*She goes to the trolley and peers behind the parcels*) Why, Henry, I believe you're right after all. It *is* a bear!

Paddington stands up suddenly. He is wearing a duffle coat, a bush hat with a wide brim and has a large luggage label round his neck

Paddington Good afternoon. (*He raises his hat*)
Mr Brown Er . . . good afternoon.
Paddington Can I help you?

Mr Brown Well . . . no. Er, not really. As a matter of fact we were wondering if *we* could help you.

Mrs Brown (*examining him closely*) You're a very unusual bear.

Paddington I'm a very *rare* sort of bear. There aren't many of us left where I come from.

Mr Brown And where is that?

Paddington Darkest Peru. I'm not really supposed to be here at all. (*After a furtive look*) I'm a stowaway.

Mrs Brown (*after a furtive look*) A stowaway?

Paddington Yes. I emigrated. I used to live with my Aunt Lucy in Peru, but she had to go into a Home for Retired Bears.

Mrs Brown You don't mean to say you've come all the way from South America by yourself?

Paddington Yes. Aunt Lucy always said she wanted me to emigrate when I was old enough. That's why she taught me to speak English.

Mr Brown But whatever did you do for food? You must be starving.

Paddington (*opening his suitcase and taking out an almost empty jar*) I ate marmalade. Bears like marmalade. And I hid in a lifeboat.

Mr Brown But what are you going to do now?

Paddington Oh, I shall be all right . . . I expect.

Mrs Brown What does it say on your label?

Mr Brown (*reading it*) "Please look after this bear. Thank you."

Mrs Brown Oh, Henry, what shall we do? We can't just leave him here. Couldn't he come and stay with us for a few days?

Mr Brown But Mary, dear, we can't take him . . . not just like that. After all . . .

Mrs Brown After all what? He'd be company for Jonathan and Judy. They'd never forgive us if they knew you'd left him *here*.

Mr Brown It all seems highly irregular. (*Turning to Paddington*) Would you like to come and stay with us? That is, if you've nothing else planned?

Paddington (*overjoyed*) Oooh, yes, please. I should like that very much.

Mrs Brown Well, that's settled then. And you can have marmalade for breakfast every morning . . .

Paddington Every morning? I only had it on special occasions at home. Marmalade's very expensive in Darkest Peru.

Mrs Brown Then you shall have it every morning—starting tomorrow.

Paddington (*worried*) Will it cost a lot? You see I haven't very much money.

Mrs Brown Of course not. We shall expect you to be one of the family shan't we, Henry?

Mr Brown (*doubtfully*) Er . . . of course. By the way, if you *are* coming home with us you'd better know our names. This is Mrs Brown . . .

Mrs Brown How d'you do . . .

Mr Brown . . . and I'm Mr Brown.

Paddington (*raises his hat twice*) I haven't really got a name, only a Peruvian one which no one can understand.

Mrs Brown Then we'd better give you an English one. It'll make things much easier. (*Thinking hard*) Now what shall we call you? I mean, what *do* you call a bear you find on Paddington Station. (*The Audience will tell her*) *Paddington*, what a good idea. We found you on Paddington Station, so that's what we'll call you . . . Paddington.

Paddington (*savouring it*) Paddington. Pad-ding-ton. Paddington. It seems a very long name.

Mr Brown It's quite distinguished. Yes, I like Paddington as a name. Paddington it shall be.

Mrs Brown Good. Oh! Look at the time. Paddington, I have to meet our daughter Judy off the train. I'm sure you must be thirsty after your long journey, so while I'm away Mr Brown will get you something to drink.

Paddington Thank you.

Mrs Brown And for goodness sake, Henry, when you get a moment, take that label off his neck. It makes him look like a parcel.

Paddington A parcel?

Paddington doesn't much like the thought of looking like a parcel

Mrs Brown We don't want someone to post you, do we?

Mrs Brown exits, almost bumping into a man pushing a refreshment trolley who enters

Paddington No!

Mr Brown It's all right. (*Removing the label*) There we are. Ah! The very thing. Now I can get you something to drink.

He hands the label to Paddington, who puts it into his suitcase

Trolley Man What would you like, *tea* or *coffee*?

Paddington Cocoa, please.

Trolley Man (*put out*) We haven't got any cocoa.

Paddington But you asked me what I would like . . .

Trolley Man I asked you what you would like, *tea* or *coffee*?

Mr Brown (*hastily, trying to avoid an argument*) Perhaps you'd like a cold drink?

Trolley Man Cold drinks, yes. Would you like *lemonade* or *orangeade*?

Paddington Marmalade.

Mr Brown (*before the man loses his temper*) I think some orangeade would be a good idea—and a cup of tea for me, please.

The Trolley Man serves them

And perhaps you'd like a cake, Paddington?

Paddington Oooh, yes, please.

Trolley Man Cream-and-chocolate, or cream-and-jam?

Paddington Thank you very much.

Trolley Man Well, which do you want?

Mr Brown We'd better have one of each.

The Trolley Man puts them on a plate. Mr Brown pays him

How's that to be going on with?

Paddington It's very nice, thank you, Mr Brown. But it's not very easy drinking out of a beaker. I usually get my nose stuck.

Mr Brown Perhaps you'd like a straw. (*He takes one from the trolley and puts it into Paddington's beaker*)

Paddington That's a good idea. (*He blows through the straw and makes a noisy bubbling sound*) Mmmm. I like that, Mr Brown.

Mr Brown (*quickly*) I'd better pour it into a saucer for you. It's not really done in the best circles, but I'm sure no one will mind just this once.

Paddington (*drinks from the saucer*) I'm glad I emigrated. (*Takes a bite from one of the cakes*) I think I'd like another one of these if I may?

He climbs up on to the rail of the refreshment trolley which tilts suddenly. He lets go hastily and it shoots across the platform bumping into a portly gentleman who pushes it back with a gesture of annoyance. It bangs into Paddington, knocking him off balance. As he flails around he upsets a tray of plastic beakers which the Trolley Man is holding, scattering them in all directions. Trying to steady himself he knocks Mr Brown's tea out of his hand, all over the Trolley Man, slips over and ends up sprawled on the platform. As Mr Brown bends to help him up Paddington staggers to his feet. They collide and Paddington's cream cake ends up plastered all over Mr Brown's face

Mrs Brown returns with Judy, both carrying usual end-of-term luggage

Mrs Brown Henry! Henry, whatever are you doing to that poor bear? Look at him! He's covered all over with jam and cream.

Mr Brown *He's* covered in jam and cream! What about me? (*He begins to tidy up the debris*)

Judy (*clapping her hands*) Oh, Daddy, is he really going to stay with us?

Mr Brown I'm not too sure at the moment . . .

Judy Oh, he *must*! (*To Paddington*) What's your name?

Paddington Er . . . oh, dear . . . I think I've forgotten . . . (*He looks to the Audience for help*)

Audience PADDINGTON!

Paddington That's it. Paddington. How do you do? (*He shakes hands with Judy*)

Mr Brown Perhaps we'd better go. (*He picks up Judy's suitcase*) Are we all ready?

Judy Come along, Paddington.

Mrs Brown You go ahead, Judy. We'll meet Jonathan and catch you up.

Judy Are you ready, Paddington?

Paddington picks up his suitcase and puts the remains of the cakes in it. The cake-wrapping sticks to his hands and he licks it happily

Paddington Yes, thank you.

Judy We'll go straight home and you can have a nice hot bath. Then you can tell me all about South America, I'm sure you must have had lots of wonderful adventures.

Paddington I have. Lots. Things are always happening to me, I'm that sort of bear.

Mr Brown (*to his wife*) I hope we haven't bitten off more than we can chew.

Trolley Man Well, if you have, you'll just have to grin and *bear* it. (*He laughs loudly at his own joke*)

Paddington gives the man a hard stare. This can be pointed with an audible effect of some kind. The man reacts and his laughter dies away

Trolley Man Sorry, sir. Very sorry indeed. (*He goes off*)

Judy Gosh! Where did you learn to do that?

Paddington My Aunt Lucy taught me. She said it might come in useful one day.

Mr Brown Do you often do it?

Paddington Only on special occasions—(*darkly*)—or when I have an emergency.

Judy We'd better get you home . . . before you have another one.

Judy goes into her song

GOING HOME (SONG)

Judy Going home
Paddington That's nice
Judy Going home
Paddington Though I liked it in Peru
I think I'll be happy here
With you
Judy It's time that we were
Going home
Together It's time that we were
Going home
We think it will be great fun
To live with a bear with a name like Paddington
Paddington I'm as happy as can be
It's nice for a bear to be with a family
All What adventures lie in store
There's no knowing
We can count on plenty more
Now we're
Going home
Paddington I'm glad I met you all today
Judy Do you think that you would like to stay
Paddington If I may
All Then
It's time that we were going home
It's time that we were going home
It's time that we were going home.

The frontcloth rises and we see number 32 Windsor Gardens. Judy and Paddington walk up to the front door

Judy Here we are. (*She knocks at the door*) Now you are going to meet Mrs Bird.
Paddington Mrs Bird?
Judy Yes. She looks after us. She's a bit fierce sometimes but she doesn't really mean it. I'm sure you'll like her.
Paddington (*nervously*) I'm sure I shall, if you say so.

The door opens and Mrs Bird appears

Mrs Bird Goodness gracious, you've arrived already. I suppose you'll be wanting tea?
Judy Hello, Mrs Bird, it's nice to see you again.
Mrs Bird (*she sees Paddington*) Good gracious! Whatever have you got there?
Judy It's not a what, Mrs Bird. It's a bear. His name's Paddington.

Paddington raises his hat

Mrs Bird A bear . . . well he has good manners, I'll say that for him.
Judy He's going to stay with us.
Mrs Bird Going to *stay* with us? For how long?
Judy I don't know. I suppose it depends on *things*.

They follow Mrs Bird into the house

Mrs Bird Mercy me. I wish you'd told me he was coming. I haven't put clean sheets in the spare room or anything.
Paddington It's all right, Mrs Bird. I'm sure I shall be very comfortable.

He shakes hands with her. When he lets go, we see that the left-over cake-wrapper is sticking to her hand. She tries in vain to get it off, and finally it sticks to her other hand

Judy Let me help, Mrs Bird. (*Judy takes it from her but then finds that it is glued to her own hand*) Paddington, would you like to shake hands with me?
Paddington Certainly.

They shake hands and the paper is transferred to Paddington's paw.

At this moment Mr and Mrs Brown arrive with Jonathan

Mr Brown Well, it didn't take us long to catch you up.
Judy Hello, Jonathan. Oh, you haven't met Paddington yet, have you. Paddington, this is my brother Jonathan.
Jonathan Wow! How do you do?
Paddington Very wow, thank you.

Paddington shakes hands with Jonathan, who collects the sticky paper.

Attempting to remove it, Mr and Mrs Brown get involved too. Eventually it gets back to Jonathan

Mrs Bird It's good to have you home, Jonathan.
Jonathan It's good to *be* home, Mrs Bird.

He shakes hands and she finds that the sticky paper has come back to her once again

Paddington Shall I take it, Mrs Bird?
Mrs Bird (*firmly*) No, thank you. I'll wash it off myself.
Paddington I'm afraid I had an accident with a cake. It's left me a bit sticky.
Mrs Bird I think a good hot bath will do you the world of good.
Judy (*confidentially*) She doesn't mind really. In fact I think she rather likes you.
Paddington She seems a bit stern.
Mrs Bird (*turning round suddenly*) What was that?
Paddington Oh! Er . . . I've got a lot to learn, Mrs Bird.
Mrs Bird (*melting*) Where was it you said you'd come from? Peru?
Paddington That's right. *Darkest* Peru.
Mrs Bird Oh! Then I expect you'd like marmalade. I'd better get some more from the grocer. (*She goes into the back of the house*)
Judy (*happily*) There you are! What did I tell you? She *does* like you.
Paddington Fancy her knowing that I like marmalade.
Judy Mrs Bird knows everything about everything.
Mrs Brown Now, Judy, you'd better show Paddington his room while Jonathan gets unpacked. (*She goes to the back of the house followed by Jonathan*)
Mr Brown And while that's going on, I'll spend a few moments on my painting. (*He moves to an easel in the corner of the room and prepares to paint*)
Paddington That looks very interesting, Mr Brown.
Judy It's for a competition. I hope you're lucky this time, Dad.
Mr Brown So do I.
Judy Come on, Paddington, and I'll show you your room. (*They go upstairs. Lights come on upstairs*) I hope you like it. It used to be mine when I was small. (*They reach the landing*) There's a shower in there so you can have a good clean up. My room is along there. (*She opens the bedroom door*) And this is going to be your room.

Paddington is very pleased with what he sees

Judy This is a chest of drawers for all of your things. Just pull the drawers out when you need them.
Paddington (*opening his suitcase*) It's very kind of you, but I haven't got very much. (*He holds up a jar*)
Judy What's that?
Paddington It's a jar of marmalade—only there's hardly any left now . . . and a scrapbook and my alarm clock.

Judy (*looking at a photograph*) And who is that?

Paddington That's a picture of my Aunt Lucy. She had it taken just before she went into the Home for Retired Bears in Lima. That's in Peru, of course.

Judy Of course. She looks very nice. And very wise.

Paddington (*a far away look in his eyes*) Oh yes, she is.

Judy (*briskly*) Well, I'm going to leave you now so that you can have your shower. You'll find two taps, one marked hot and one marked cold. There's plenty of soap and a clean towel. Oh, and a brush so that you can scrub your back.

Paddington It sounds very complicated. Can't I just sit in a puddle or something.

Judy Sit in a puddle. (*She laughs*) I don't think Mrs Bird would approve of that. And don't forget to wash your ears. They look awfully black. (*She goes out, down the stairs and into the kitchen*)

Paddington (*calling after her*) They're meant to be black! Now what next? Oh, yes, I'll put my things away in the chest of drawers. What did Judy say? Just pull them out when you need them. (*He pulls the handles of the first drawer, which to his surprise comes completely out. He puts his belongings into it and puts it under the bed*) Now I'd better have a shower, I suppose. (*He goes through the door, into the shower cubicle and draws the curtain. A moment later he opens the curtain again and looks out*) It's all wet! It's a good thing I've got my hat.

He pulls his hat firmly down over his ears and goes back inside the shower, pulling the curtain behind him. As the shower spray begins the Lights dim and come up on Mr and Mrs Brown and Jonathan. Judy joins them in the sitting-room

Mr Brown I hope we're doing the right thing.

Mrs Brown Well, we can hardly turn him out now. It wouldn't be fair.

Mr Brown Well, we'll have to see what Mrs Bird has to say about it first.

Jonathan Hurrah!

The door opens and Mrs Bird enters the sitting-room from the kitchen carrying a tray of tea. She pauses and looks at their expectant faces

Judy Now's your chance to ask her.

Mrs Bird I suppose you want to tell me you've decided to keep that young Paddington.

Judy May we, Mrs Bird? *Please*. I'm sure he'll be very good.

Mrs Bird Humph! (*She puts the tray on the table*) I must say he looks the sort of bear who means well.

Mr Brown Then you don't mind, Mrs Bird?

Mrs Bird No. No, I don't mind at all. I've always had a soft spot for bears myself. It'll be nice to have one about the house.

Mrs Brown By the way, where is Paddington?

Judy Oh, he's all right. He's just having a shower.

All Oh? Good. That's all right, etc.

A noisy bubbling sound. The Lights come up on the shower. Paddington has blocked up the waste hole with a flannel and foaming water is beginning to overflow. Steam rises from all around. He is singing to himself, oblivious of the mess he is causing. The water is up to his chest and rising. Mr Brown is seated underneath with his painting and some drops fall on his head

Mr Brown That's funny. I could have sworn I felt a drop of water.
Mrs Brown Don't be silly, Henry. How could you?
Mr Brown (*another drop lands on his head*) It's happened again!
Jonathan (*looks up and sees what is happening*) Crikey! Water!
Judy Oh gosh. The shower!
Jonathan Come on!
Mr Brown Where are you two going?
Judy Oh—(*pretending to be casual*)—just upstairs to see how Paddington's getting on. (*She bundles Jonathan out of the room and up the stairs*) Hurry!
Mrs Brown (*taking out the tea tray*) What was all that about, I wonder?
Mr Brown (*following her*) I suppose they're excited at having a bear about the house . . .

They go into the kitchen

Judy (*as she gets to the shower*) Are you all right, Paddington?
Paddington Glug! Glug! Help! Help! Yes, I think so.
Judy Oh, dear. Get the water out.
Jonathan There! (*He pulls out Paddington's flannel*) Didn't you know you'd got the flannel over the plug-hole?
Paddington The water kept running away.
Jonathan It's meant to. That's the whole idea of a shower. Wow! (*Impressed*) Fancy making all this mess.
Paddington Oh, it was quite easy.
Judy Now you just dry yourself properly or you'll catch cold.
Paddington (*proudly*) I'm a lot cleaner than I was.
Judy You'd better give me your hat and I'll put it in the airing cupboard to dry out.
Paddington I'd rather you didn't. I don't like to be without it. It's my special bush hat.
Judy Oh, come along, Paddington. (*Taking him to his room*) Now that you're clean, will you tell us about yourself and how you came to emigrate.
Paddington (*sitting on his bed and making the most of his audience*) Well . . . I was brought up by my Aunt Lucy. (*He closes his eyes*)
Jonathan Your Aunt Lucy?
Paddington Yes. She's the one who lives in the Home for Retired Bears in (*snore*)—ima . . .
Jonathan In SNORE-ima! Where's that?
Paddington It's in Peru. (*Snore*) *Darkest* Peru.
Judy Paddington!

He gives a longer snore

Oh dear!

Jonathan It looks as if we'll have to wait until tomorrow for the rest of the story.

Judy I expect he's had a tiring day—what with one thing and another.

Judy tucks him up into bed

JUDY'S LULLABY (SONG)

Now he's sleeping
Safe in our keeping
We've got our very own Paddington Bear
Drowsing, yawning
Sound asleep till morning
Shall we all look after this bear.
What an unusual situation
Finding a bear on a railway station
What an astonishing thing for a bear to do
Stowing away in a lifeboat from darkest Peru
Soundly sleeping
Safe in our keeping
We've got our very own Paddington Bear
So children, please look after this bear.

The Lights dim

The following morning. Paddington is still asleep. Mr and Mrs Brown and Jonathan are finishing breakfast. Mr Brown puts down the morning paper

Mr Brown Pass the marmalade, please, Mary.

Mrs Brown Would you mind having honey instead? There isn't much marmalade left and I'm sure Paddington will want some when he comes down to breakfast.

Mr Brown Yes, of course. (*He returns to his paper*)

Mrs Brown I think I'd better order a seven-pound tin.

An alarm-clock rings. Paddington stirs. He pulls the blankets over his head so that his feet stick out of the bottom of the bed. He wiggles his toes then turns around under the bedclothes and sticks his head out of the wrong end of the bed. He yawns, gets up and opens the curtains. The sun streams in.

Paddington That was a strange dream. I thought I was found on a railway station and brought to live with a family at number thirty-two Windsor Gardens. Except I can't remember the name of the station . . . (*The Audience tell him*) Paddington! It wasn't a dream after all! (*He sniffs the air appreciatively*) And that's another thing that isn't a dream. I can smell breakfast.

Paddington opens the bedroom door and comes downstairs backwards. Judy runs upstairs and collides with him

Paddington Good morning, Judy.

Judy Good morning, Paddington. Are you coming or going?
Mrs Brown Good morning, Paddington.
Paddington Good morning, Mrs Brown. Good morning, Mr Brown. Hello, Jonathan.
Mr Brown Good morning, Paddington. Did you sleep well?
Paddington Oh, yes. Very well, thank you.
Mrs Brown You'd better sit down and have your breakfast.
Paddington Thank you.

Mr Brown passes Paddington a boiled egg which he puts into his mouth whole

It's very crunchy, Mr Brown.
Mr Brown Er . . . yes. (*Looking at his watch*) Well, I'd better be off now or I'll be late for work. (*He rises*)
Mrs Brown Good-bye, dear.

Mr Brown exits

Paddington (*testing the marmalade*) This is very chunky marmalade. It's even better than the sort I used to get—in Darkest Peru.
Judy That's good. It's some of Mrs Bird's special home-made.
Jonathan Talking of Mrs Bird, I'd better go and finish unpacking—otherwise she'll be after me.
Judy Gosh, yes. I've still got masses. What would you like to do, Paddington?
Paddington I haven't got very much to unpack. (*Brightly*) Perhaps I could go and buy a frame for Aunt Lucy's photograph. Then I could hang it up.
Jonathan I bet you'd get one in Mr Gruber's antique shop. He's got everything.
Mrs Brown Do you think it's a good idea to let Paddington go out all by himself on his first morning?
Judy It's only just around the corner.
Jonathan It's not far enough for anything to go wrong. You can't miss it . . . look for the sign saying Portobello Road. Mr Gruber's shop's on the left going down.

Paddington gets up to leave

Mrs Brown Well, don't be too long. And mind you go carefully. (*She goes into the kitchen*)
Jonathan (*calling after Paddington as he leaves*) You can borrow my roller skates if you like. Then you'll be twice as quick.
Judy Oh, Jonathan. Really! (*She goes upstairs*) He's only got paws.
Jonathan (*calling after her*) It was just a joke.

Paddington is outside by now. He sees Jonathan's roller skates standing by the front door

Paddington Roller skates! Mmm. I don't think I've ever tried any of those before.

Paddington decides to test the skates. He puts one on his left paw, then stands on his right one and tries to push off with the left. When this fails he puts the other skate on his right paw. He stands up on both skates looking very pleased with himself

Paddington Paws on wheels! I like this . . .

He falls over

I think.

He stands up

Perhaps I've got them on the wrong paws.

He has another go, but this time he puts them on his front paws and heads off down the road on all fours

Mr Curry enters reading his morning newspaper and as they collide he is knocked off balance

Mr Curry What's going on? Why don't you look where you're going?
Paddington (*raising his hat from a sitting position*) I'm sorry, Mr . . .
Mr Curry Curry's the name.
Paddington I'm very sorry, Mr Curry. Can I help you up?

He tries to help Mr Curry to his feet, but at the crucial moment he steps on one of the skates and they end up on the pavement again

Mr Curry Bear! What are you doing, bear? (*He peers hard at Paddington*) Who *are* you, anyway?
Paddington I'm Paddington. (*He looks round to make sure he can't be overheard and then puts his mouth to Mr Curry's ear*) I come from Darkest Peru, but Mr and Mrs Brown are letting me stay at number thirty-two Windsor Gardens.
Mr Curry Number thirty-two? But that's next door to me. Nobody's asked my permission. I've a good mind to . . . (*He breaks off and feels his ear. He removes something from it*) Ugh! What's this?

Paddington peers at it. Touches it with his paw and then tastes it

Paddington I think it's a marmalade chunk, Mr Curry. Some of Mrs Bird's special. I expect it got left on at breakfast. It must have fallen in your ear by mistake.
Mr Curry A marmalade chunk? In my ear? Pah! You may be staying next door, bear, but if you know what's good for you, you'll stay out of my sight from now on.

He stands up, stamps his foot angrily, steps on the roller skates and falls over again

Paddington exits hurriedly

Mr Curry turns and glares at the Audience as he stands and goes into his song

MR CURRY'S GRUMBLING SONG

So you think that bears are most amusing creatures
Well, they may be when they're in their proper place
But I'd rather do hard labour
Than have *that* one for a neighbour
It's a *scandal.* It's not *right*. It's a disgrace.
I think it most improper!
A bear like that should be inside a zoo.
A man like me won't wear it
I refuse to grin and bear it
For I don't like bears
Do you?

YES.

Oh, I don't like bears
I don't like bears
Nasty little rare bears from Peru
I don't like bears, I don't like bears, I don't like bears
Do you?

YES.

It's not a very happy situation
Surely decent people will agree?
It's absolutely awful
And it should be made unlawful
For a bear like that to make a fool of me.
It's quite absurd. It's shocking.
Surely there is *something* I can do.
A man like me won't wear it
I refuse to grin and bear it
For I don't like bears
Do you?

YES.

Oh, I don't like bears
I don't like bears
Nasty little rare bears from Peru
I don't like bears, I don't like bears, I don't like bears
Do you?

YES.

Music

Mr Gruber's antique shop in the Portobello Road. He is cleaning an oil painting when Paddington arrives

Mr Gruber Good morning. Can I help you?

Paddington (*putting down his suitcase*) I've got some important shopping to do and you were recommended.

Mr Gruber Really? How nice! Was there anything in particular you were wanting?

Paddington My Aunt Lucy needs a frame. About—(*he shows him*)—*this* big.

Mr Gruber What sort of frame would she like?

Paddington Oh, *she* doesn't want it. It's for her photograph. She lives in a Home for Retired Bears in Lima.

Mr Gruber I see. I think I may have the very thing, Mr . . .

Paddington Brown. Paddington Brown. I come from Darkest Peru, but I'm staying at number thirty-two Windsor Gardens.

Mr Gruber Number thirty-two Windsor Gardens! I know that very well. I must find something special for you in that case. Here you are . . . (*He hands Paddington a frame*) Slightly damaged on one corner, but it's very good otherwise. It's yours for twenty pence.

Paddington (*examining it carefully*) Oh, dear, I've only got Peruvian money.

Mr Gruber Take it. You can pay me when you're next passing by. Any friend of the Browns is a friend of mine.

Paddington Thank you very much, Mr Gruber.

Mr Gruber I've just made some cocoa, Mr Brown. Would you care for a cup?

Paddington Cocoa! Yes, please.

Mr Gruber It's quite hot. I keep it in a vacuum.

Paddington (*amazed*) You keep your cocoa in a vacuum cleaner?

Mr Gruber No, a vacuum flask. (*He pours some cocoa and hands it to Paddington*) There's nothing like a chat over a bun and a cup of cocoa.

Paddington A bun as well! That's very kind of you.

They sit down to enjoy their elevenses

What were you doing when I came into the shop, Mr Gruber?

Mr Gruber I was cleaning a painting. (*He picks it up*) Now, what do you think of that?

Paddington (*looking at it*) It's a puzzle, Mr Gruber, one half is a boat and the other half is a lady in a large hat. Has she fallen out of the boat?

Mr Gruber (*laughing*) No, Mr Brown. As a matter of fact she was there first. I gave five shillings for that painting years ago when it was just a picture of a sailing ship. And what do you think? When I started to clean it the other day, all the paint began to come off and I discovered that there was another painting underneath. It could be an old master.

Paddington An old master? It looks like an old lady to me.

Mr Gruber Yes, but painted by a famous artist. It could be very valuable.

Paddington That sounds very interesting. Very interesting indeed. (*He gets up, his mind obviously elsewhere*) I'll have to be going now, Mr Gruber. Thank you for the elevenses.

Mr Gruber Is anything the matter, Mr Brown?

Paddington No, Mr Gruber. I've had an idea, that's all. (*Mysteriously, as* *he makes to leave*) I may be able to pay you for the picture frame sooner than I thought.

Mr Gruber Good day, Mr Brown.

Paddington exits

(*He watches Paddington go*) Now, I wonder what he meant by that?

Music

The Brown's sitting-room. The table is partly laid with various condiments. A large tube of mustard, tomato sauce, marmalade, etc. Paddington comes in, looks round carefully and closes the door behind him. He takes off his duffle coat and producing a bottle of paint remover from his pocket, bears down on Mr Brown's painting. He soaks a handkerchief in paint remover and rubs it over the painting. He stands back to look and is horrified by what he sees, decides to have another try and is giving the painting a vigorous scrub when he is interrupted by the entry of Mrs Bird

Mrs Bird Paddington! What *are* you up to? I thought you'd gone to see Mr Gruber.

Paddington I did, Mrs Bird. But I'm back now. (*Gloomily*) I wish I wasn't! Can I get you anything from the shops?

Mrs Bird (*seeing the picture*) What *have* you been doing? That's Mr Brown's painting that he did specially for the competition.

Paddington I know. I've been cleaning it. I thought there might be an old master underneath.

Mrs Bird An old master? (*She looks at the painting*) It used to be some boats on a lake, now it looks like a storm at sea.

Paddington Oh, dear.

Mrs Bird I don't know, I'm sure. I think it's best if I haven't seen it. (*She goes to leave the room and pauses at the door. She talks away from Paddington*) Mind you, if I'd got myself in a mess like that I think I might try my paw at putting it right . . . But don't say I said so.

Paddington Oh, I shan't, Mrs Bird. Thank you very much.

Mrs Bird Don't be too long. They're supposed to be coming for it this morning.

Mrs Bird exits

Paddington This morning! But I haven't got any paints! (*But it is too late—Mrs Bird had already gone. He picks up a brush and looks around for inspiration*) Perhaps I'd better make do. (*He sees the condiments on the table, picks up a tube of mustard and squeezes it on to the painting. Then rubs it with the brush*) Mustard . . . makes a nice, yellow colour. I'll try some tomato sauce. (*He does so*) And there's nothing like a spot of marmalade.

He enters into the whole affair with gusto, and if the painting isn't improved, at least it is very "different".

At the appropriate moment a Lady arrives to collect the picture. She knocks on the door

Paddington comes down to earth with a bump as he answers the door

The Lady Good afternoon! I believe Mr Brown has a picture he's entering for our show. I've called to collect it.
Paddington Oh, dear! You wouldn't like to come back next week?
The Lady I'm afraid not. The final judging takes place this afternoon.
Paddington The *final* judging?

He goes back to the sitting-room, gives the painting a finishing dab, wipes his brush on his hat, drops the painting into a canvas bag and takes it to the front door

The Lady Thank you very much. The judges will be awarding the prizes today. I expect you will hear the results later this evening. Good-bye.

The Lady exits

Paddington Good-bye. (*He looks around the room*) I think I've gone off painting. I bet the old masters never had this much trouble!

Music

Later that day. The Brown family are finishing dinner

Mrs Brown Would you like a cup of cocoa, Paddington?
Paddington No, thank you.
Mrs Brown Are you all right?
Paddington Yes, I thank so, think you. I mean, I think so, thank you.

He goes upstairs to his room where he sits on the bed with a worried look on his face

Mrs Brown I do hope he's all right, Henry. He seemed to have funny red spots all over his face.
Jonathan Red spots! I wonder if it's measles? I hope he's given it to me, whatever it is. Then I shan't have to go back to school.
Judy Well, he's got green ones as well. I distinctly saw them.
Mr Brown Green ones! Well, if they're not gone in the morning we'd better send for the doctor.
Jonathan They're judging the paintings today, aren't they, Dad?
Mr Brown Yes, they took mine away this afternoon.
Jonathan Do you think you'll win a prize?
Mrs Brown No-one will be more surprised than your father if he does. He's never won anything yet.
Judy I wonder if Paddington's feeling any better?
Jonathan Perhaps they have *green* measles in Darkest Peru.

Judy goes upstairs

As Judy reaches the landing an arty-looking Man with a beard arrives at the front door accompanied by the Lady who collected the painting earlier. The Man is carrying the painting which is still in its canvas bag

The Lady This is it. (*She knocks*)
Mrs Bird All right, I'm just coming. (*She goes to the door*)
The Man I wonder if we might see Mr Brown? It's about the painting he did.
Mrs Bird Oh, dear, I suppose you'd better. (*She leads them into the sitting-room*)
Judy (*on the stairs—as Paddington's door opens*) Paddington, you look most peculiar. Are you all right?
Paddington I don't feel ill, but I think I'm in trouble again.
Judy Well, don't worry. Nothing is as black as it's painted.
Paddington (*gloomily*) I think mine is!
Mrs Bird Will you come in here, please?
The Man Mr Brown?
Mr Brown That's right.
The Man I'm the President of the Art Society and this is Miss Block who is one of the judges of the competition.
Mr Brown How do you do?
The Man I've some news for you.
Paddington Ooooh! Ooh!
The Man Is that a cow mooing?
Mrs Bird No, sir. I think it's a bear oooohing.
The Man (*astonished*) Oh! Mr Brown, I've some very good news for you. The judges decided that your painting was most unusual.
Mrs Bird (*aside*) It certainly was.
The Man And without hesitation, they decided to award the first prize to you.
Mr Brown The *first* prize?
Miss Block Yes, they thought your painting showed great imagination.
Mr Brown (*pleased*) Did they now?
The Man Yes. It made great use of marmalade chunks.
The Browns (*chorus*) Marmalade chunks!
The Man Yes, and tomato sauce, and mustard and all sorts of things. I don't think I've ever come across anything quite like it before. (*He places the painting on the easel, removing the cover as he does so*) It is, to say the least, unusual. More a collage of sauces, paints and marmalade chunks than a painting. There you are!
Jonathan I didn't know you were interested in abstract art, Dad.
Mr Brown Nor did I!

Paddington and Judy creep downstairs and listen round the corner

Miss Block What are you calling it?
Mr Brown Where's Paddington?
Miss Block Where's Paddington? What a funny title.
The Man Well, sir, my congratulations! Just one more thing . . . your

prize. (*He hands over a cheque*) First prize to Mr Henry Brown . . . ten pounds. What will you do with it, may I ask, Mr Brown?

Mr Brown (*wearily*) I think I shall give half to someone not too far away at this present moment and the rest I shall donate to a certain Home for Retired Bears in South America.

The Man Oh, really? Well, we must be getting along.

They exit and Paddington and Judy enter the room

Mrs Bird Well, Paddington. What have you got to say for yourself?

Paddington (*crossing to the easel*) I think they might have stood it the right way up. (*He turns the picture upright*) It's not every day a bear wins first prize in a painting competition.

Mr Brown I'm still not sure what happened.

Paddington I was looking for an old master, Mr Brown.

Mr Brown An old master. It looks more like a young bear to me. Marmalade chunks! I've never heard of such a thing.

Judy Oh, I don't know. I'll say one thing for it.

Jonathan What's that?

Judy (*removing a marmalade chunk from the picture and with a flourish puts it into her mouth*) It not only looks good . . . it *tastes* good!

Judy goes into song

MARMALADE SONG

Judy What does a bear like Paddington do
When he's sad and feeling blue?
What does a bear like Paddington say
To make those bear blues go away?
He says marmalade

Paddington It's good to eat
Marmalade
What a lovely treat
There's nothing makes a meal complete
Like marmalade

Audience *Marmalade!*

Paddington I like marmalade of every kind
Thick or jelly, chunks or rind
Lemon, Orange, I don't mind
If it's marmalade

Audience *Marmalade!*

Paddington And sometimes when I sit and dream
I think of places where
The sandwiches are extra thick
And nearly five feet square
I'd love a jar of marmalade
Just any sort at all
As long as it was really full
And over ten feet tall

So if you're gloomy or in doubt
And when your luck is running out
All you have to do is shout
Marmalade!

Audience *Marmalade!*

Mr Gruber's shop in Portobello Road. Mr Gruber is polishing an old candlestick when Paddington arrives

Mr Gruber Good morning, Mr Brown.

Paddington Good morning, Mr Gruber.

Mr Gruber You've chosen a good time to call.

Paddington Have I?

Mr Gruber Yes, it's just eleven o'clock.

Paddington (*looking at his alarm clock*) So it is. There's something else as well.

Mr Gruber What's that?

Paddington I've got the twenty pence I owe you for the picture frame. Mr Brown won first prize in a painting competition and he gave half of it to me.

Mr Gruber Thank you very much. I take it you'll stay to cocoa?

Paddington Yes, please. (*He takes the cup which Mr Gruber offers*) What's that you're polishing?

Mr Gruber It's an antique candlestick. It's over one hundred years old and it's worth about twenty pounds.

Paddington Twenty pounds! I should have thought you could have bought a new one for that.

Mr Gruber It wouldn't be the same, Mr Brown. It's valuable because it's been handed down. It's what's known as an heirloom.

Paddington Like my hat?

Mr Gruber Well, something like, yes. Was the picture frame a success?

Paddington Yes, it fitted very well, thank you. Mr Gruber, do you like parties?

Mr Gruber Well, I don't go to very many, Mr Brown, but I always enjoy them when I do.

Paddington I'm having one tonight. Can you come?

Mr Gruber I'd be delighted, Mr Brown. Is it your birthday?

Paddington Yes, it's my summer one, Mr Gruber.

Mr Gruber Your *summer* one?

Paddington I have one in the winter as well. Bears have two birthdays every year, like the Queen.

Mr Gruber I see. Well, I shall look forward to it very much indeed. What time shall I come?

Paddington About four o'clock, Mr Gruber.

Mr Gruber Right. I've got something in here which you might like to accept as a birthday present. It isn't absolutely new but it's very unusual. (*He brings a large cardboard box from the back of the shop*)

Paddington Thank you very much, Mr Gruber. What is it?

Mr Gruber It's a conjuring set.

Paddington A conjuring set! Just what I've always wanted.

Mr Gruber I know it isn't your birthday party until this evening, but if you take it home with you now, you'll have a chance to practice some of the tricks. Then you can entertain everybody.

Paddington What a good idea. Thank you very much, Mr Gruber. And thank you for the cocoa. I'll see you this evening. (*He goes, taking the box with him*)

Mr Gruber Good day, Mr Brown. Don't forget, read the instructions carefully.

Music

The Browns' sitting-room. The framed picture of Paddington's Aunt Lucy occupies a place of honour on the sideboard. Mrs Bird is laying the table

Mrs Brown Is everything ready, Mrs Bird?

Mrs Bird Yes. (*Putting the candle on the cake*) Now, how many will there be? You and Mr Brown, Jonathan, Judy and Paddington—that's five, then Mr Gruber and me, that's seven.

Mrs Brown And Mr Curry.

Mrs Bird That old grumbler. I didn't know he'd been invited.

Mrs Brown He hasn't really. He invited himself.

Mrs Bird Just because there's a free tea. And I expect he'll even complain about that.

Mrs Brown I'm afraid you may be right. But it was very difficult once he'd invited himself along.

Mrs Bird I think it's disgusting, taking the crumbs off a young bear's plate like that.

Mrs Brown He'll have to look slippy if he expects to get any crumbs off Paddington's plate.

Judy (*coming in*) And he didn't even bother to wish Paddington many happy returns.

Mrs Brown Perhaps he will when the party starts.

Jonathan (*coming in*) It's four o'clock, isn't anybody here yet?

A knock at the front door as Mr Gruber arrives, closely followed by Mr Curry

Mrs Brown There's somebody now.

Paddington It's all right, Mrs Bird, I'll go. (*He comes downstairs and opens the front door*) Hello, Mr Gruber, hello, Mr Curry, please come in. (*He greets them by honking a tune on a toy trumpet*)

Mr Gruber Thank you, Mr Brown.

Mr Curry Thank you, bear. (*They go into the sitting-room*)

Mrs Brown Hello, it's very kind of you both to come.

Jonathan Where's Dad?

Mr Brown (*appearing from the kitchen*) Here I am! Hello, Mr Gruber. Hello, Mr Curry.
Mr Gruber Good evening.
Mr Curry 'Evening.
Mr Brown Well now, we all know why we're here.
Paddington Yes!
Mr Brown Because it's Paddington's birthday.
Jonathan Hurrah!

Jonathan leads them all in singing "Happy Birthday"

Paddington That's very kind of you all. I didn't know there was a special Paddington birthday song. (*He puts the trumpet down on a chair*)
Mr Brown And now, before we light the candle and get down to the real business of the evening which is——
Paddington Marmalade sandwiches!
Mr Brown —and birthday cake. If you'll all be seated I think Paddington has a surprise for us.

Mr Curry sits down, but jumps up again immediately when he finds that he has landed on the toy trumpet. Paddington goes into the kitchen and returns carrying the conjuror's table and wearing a top hat. He sets the table up beside Mr Curry

Paddington (*waving his hand for silence after consulting his instruction book*) Ladies and gentlemen, my next trick is impossible.
Mr Curry Your *next* trick, but you haven't done one yet!
Paddington (*pointedly ignoring the interruption*) For this trick I shall require an egg.
Mrs Bird Oh, dear! (*She goes to the kitchen to get one*)
Mrs Brown I feel sure something dreadful is going to happen.
Jonathan He looks good doesn't he? I wonder if he's got a rabbit inside his hat.
Mrs Bird (*returning with the egg*) Here you are.
Paddington (*taking it with a slight bow*) Thank you. I now place the egg in the centre of my magic table and cover it with the cloth, so. (*To Jonathan*) Now, sir, you're quite sure the egg is there?
Jonathan Absolutely sure.
Paddington Good. (*He waves his wand*) Abracadabra! (*He lifts the cloth and the egg has disappeared*)
Jonathan That's very good!
Judy I wonder how he does it.
Mr Curry It's quite easy really. It's all done by sleight of paw. Not bad though, for a bear. But can you bring it back again?
Paddington (*putting the cloth back over the table*) Abracadabra! Now, ladies and gentlemen, when I lift the cloth you will see that the egg has returned. (*He whisks away the cloth and is surprised to find a jar of marmalade instead*) That's funny!
Mr Curry Oh, yes. Very funny. Making us think you were going to find an egg and it was a jar of marmalade all the time!

Mr Gruber Very good, Mr Brown. (*They all clap*)
Paddington (*after taking a bow*) Thank you. For my next trick, I need a watch.
Mr Brown (*anxiously*) Are you sure? Wouldn't anything else do?
Paddington (*consulting the book*) It says here a watch.
Mr Curry Here you are, bear, I'll lend you mine. Only it's very valuable, so look after it.
Paddington Thank you, Mr Curry. (*He places it on the table*) This is a very good trick. (*He covers the watch with the cloth*) Now, I take this hammer—(*he takes a hammer from the box*)—and I hit the watch with it, so! (*He hammers the watch*)
Mr Curry (*rising*) I hope you know what you're doing, young bear.
Paddington Of course. (*He hits it again*) Now, Mr Curry, perhaps you'll lift the cloth for me.

Mr Curry lifts the cloth and sees his battered watch

Mr Curry What's this?
Paddington It doesn't look very good, does it? I think I forgot to say abracadabra.
Mr Curry Abracadabra! *Abracadabra!* (*He snatches up the remains of the watch*) Twenty years I've had this watch, and now look at it. Shock-proof . . .
Mr Brown It doesn't look very shockproof to me.
Mr Curry Seventeen jewels!
Paddington (*sweeping up some of the remains and handing them to Mr Curry*) Here are *some* of them, Mr Curry.
Mr Curry Pah!
Mr Gruber May I see that watch a moment. (*He takes out an eyeglass*)
Mr Curry You may—what's left of it!
Mr Gruber There may not be much left, Mr Curry, but I know one of my own watches when I see it. You bought this from me for fifty pence not six months ago!
Mr Curry Rubbish! (*To Paddington*) I've had enough of your silly tricks. (*He sits down heavily in an armchair*) Pah! (*His face changes as a fresh disaster strikes*) I'm sitting on something wet and sticky.
Paddington Oh, dear, I expect it's my disappearing egg. It must have re-appeared.
Mr Curry (*rising furiously*) I've never been so insulted in my life. Never! (*He points an accusing finger at the company*) It's the last time I shall ever come to one of *your* birthday parties.

Mr Curry exits, banging the door behind himself

Mr Brown begins to laugh

Mrs Brown Henry, you really oughtn't to laugh.
Mr Brown It's no good, I can't help it.
Judy (*joining in*) Did you see his face when he sat on the egg?
Jonathan We shall be able to have an omelet for supper!

By this time they are all helpless with laughter

Mr Gruber I'm sure the man who invented that trick never saw it performed better.

Paddington I'm glad you enjoyed it. Would you like me to do another disappearing trick?

Mr Brown (*hastily*) No, thank you. The secret of success as an entertainer is to leave the audience wanting more.

Mrs Bird (*lighting the candle*) I suggest we try and make the cake disappear instead.

Judy You must blow out the candle, Paddington, and make a wish.

Paddington I wish . . .

Jonathan No, you mustn't tell your wish to anybody.

Paddington All right. I wish (*He thinks a wish*) I wish . . . (*He blows out the candle*)

Mr Gruber Happy birthday, Mr Brown.

They all cheer

Paddington Yes, it is. A very happy birthday. What shall we do now?

Jonathan How about singing us the song I heard you practising yesterday?

Paddington My song about Noah's Ark?

Judy Yes, that's the one.

Paddington I'd like to. Except I shall need some help with the chorus.

All Of course we will, etc. . . .

Mr Brown (*to the Audience*) And will you all join in, too?

PADDINGTON'S NOAH'S ARK SONG

Paddington When Noah built the Ark
He told his family
To call on all the animals
So they could go to sea.
They called on all the jungle beasts
The birds and insects too
From here, from there, from everywhere
They all joined in the queue.
The mouse, the dog, the louse, the frog
The rabbit followed the skunk
The zebra used the crossing
And the elephant brought his trunk
The kitten said "miaow, miaow"
The owl "tu wit tu woo"
And this is what the others said
Joining in the queue . . .

Audience Tweet tweet, quack quack, oink oink, cluck cluck,
buzz buzz, woof woof, cockadoodledoo.

Paddington The bull came out of the china shop
The badger followed the mole

The bumble-bee said "wait for me"
And the toad came out of his hole.
The donkey said "he haw, he haw"
And startled the kangaroo
And this is what the others said
Joining in the queue . . .

Audience Tweet tweet, quack quack, oink oink, cluck cluck, buzz buzz, woof woof, cockadoodledoo.

Paddington The cats, the goats, the gnats, the stoats,
The magpies came with the rooks
The leopard even changed his spots
And the puffins brought their books.
The little lambs said "baa, baa, baa"
The dove said "coo, coo, coo"
And this is what the others said
Joining in the queue . . .

Audience Tweet tweet, quack quack, oink oink, cluck cluck, buzz buzz, woof woof, cockadoodledoo.

Everybody joins in and after a rousing final chorus, they all clap as—

the CURTAIN *falls*

ACT II

The Browns' sitting-room

Mrs Bird is putting two piles of washing into plastic bags. Paddington enters as she checks the various articles against a list

Mrs Bird Four pairs of socks, two woollen vests, one pair of long combinations . . .

Paddington Hello, Mrs Bird.

Mrs Bird Two shirts, four pillowcases and one tablecloth. Hello, Paddington. I must hurry, I want to catch the laundry-man.

Paddington I'm afraid it's too late, Mrs Bird. He's already been. He went down the street about ten minutes ago.

Mrs Bird Isn't that annoying. Now what shall I do? These things must be washed today and I have to go out.

Paddington Can I take them to the launderette for you, Mrs Bird? Mr Gruber told me all about them. He says you just put the clothes in the machines and you sit and watch them going round and round. He says its better than watching television sometimes.

Mrs Bird Well, I don't know. I've got some of Mr Curry's things as well. He left them for the laundry-man. Some socks and his long combinations.

Paddington I don't mind taking Mr Curry's clothes.

Mrs Bird Are you sure you can manage?

Paddington Quite sure, Mrs Bird.

Mrs Bird Perhaps you could give your hat a wash at the same time. It's got a lot of stains on it.

Paddington (*indignantly*) Wash my hat! These stains have been handed down.

Mrs Bird (*hastily*) You'll need some money. (*She hands it to him*) I've given you some extra. You'll find there's a small machine on the wall of the launderette. If you put five pence in the slot, you'll get a good hot cup of cocoa so you can have your elevenses while the clothes are being washed.

Paddington Thank you very much, Mrs Bird.

Mrs Bird And perhaps you would like to take a sandwich as well. (*She hands him a sandwich*)

Paddington (*putting the sandwich inside his hat*) Thank you, Mrs Bird.

Mrs Bird Thank *you*, Paddington.

Paddington tucks a bundle under each arm, goes to the front door. Puts them down to open it, picks them up again and finds that he cannot get through the door. Eventually he goes into the kitchen and returns with the washing in a wheelbarrow which he pushes down the steps into the street

Music

The Launderette. There is a row of washing machines visible. Various customers are waiting for their washing. As many as can double up with other parts. The Lady Attendant puts down her magazine as Paddington comes through the door

Attendant Come in, dear. My, you look as if you've got the washing for the whole street!

Paddington Oh, no, it's for Mrs Bird.

Attendant *Mrs* Bird? (*She holds up Mr Curry's long combinations*)

Paddington Yes. And Mr Curry, of course. (*He gives her a hard stare*)

Attendant (*reacting*) Oh, of course! Well, I'm afraid you'll need two machines for this lot. I'll give you number eleven and twelve. Do you know how to work them?

Paddington I think so. Bears are good at instructions.

Attendant (*she places four beakers of detergent on a nearby tray*) That's two beakers for each machine. You put the first lot in when it starts and the second lot when the buzzer sounds.

Paddington Thank you very much.

The Attendant exits

Mr Gruber enters

Mr Gruber Why, hello, Mr Brown. I didn't expect to see you here.

Paddington Hello, Mr Gruber, I'm very pleased to see you.

Mr Gruber Why, what's the matter?

Paddington I didn't know I was going to have *two* machines, and I'm not sure which bundle of washing should go in the hot wash and which in the warm wash.

Mr Gruber Oh, I expect I can help you there. (*He examines the bundles*) All of these go into the hot wash, and this bundle goes into the warm wash. (*He places them carefully on the floor*) The bundle on the *left* goes in the hot and this bundle on the *right* goes into the warm. That's easy to remember isn't it?

Paddington (*standing behind them facing the entrance*) Oh, yes, thank you. Left hot. Right warm. (*He indicates with his paws*)

Mr Gruber You must get it the right way round or some of the clothes will shrink and others will stretch.

Paddington Have you finished your washing for today?

Mr Gruber Oh, yes. I'm just going home. Perhaps you would like to drop in for elevenses on your way home?

Paddington It's very kind of you, Mr Gruber, but I expect I'll get some cocoa from the machine.

COCOA SAMBA (SONG)

Paddington Have a cup of cocoa
Nice cup of cocoa

Others Have a cup of cocoa
Have a cup of cocoa
Paddington Lovely cocoa, steaming hot
There's nothing nicer than a spot
Of cocoa
Others Have a cup of cocoa
Please come and have a cup of cocoa with me,
Cocoa, cocoa, cocoa, cocoa, cocoa, cocoa, cocoa,
Cocoa, cocoa, cocoa, cocoa, cocoa, cocoa, cocoa,
Mr Gruber &
Paddington Lots of people say they like
Coffee at eleven
But drinking cocoa any time is
My idea of heaven.
Later in the afternoon
Others take their tea
But I really think the only drink for me me me
Is a cup of cocoa
Others Just a cup of cocoa
Lovely cocoa, steaming hot
There's nothing better than a spot
Of cocoa
Just a cup of cocoa
Paddington So come and have a cup of cocoa with me.
Cocoa, cocoa, cocoa, cocoa, cocoa, cocoa, cocoa.
Cocoa, cocoa, cocoa, cocoa, cocoa, cocoa, cocoa.
Cocoa, cocoa, cocoa, cocoa, cocoa, cocoa, cocoa.
Cocoa, cocoa, cocoa, cocoa, cocoa, cocoa, cocoa.
Come and have a cup of cocoa with me.
Others Champagne makes me want to sing
Paddington It only makes me dizzy
Others How about some lemonade?
Paddington I find it rather fizzy.
But give me cocoa and I'm just as happy as can be
I really think the only drink for me me me
Is a cup of cocoa
Just a cup of cocoa.
All Lovely cocoa, steaming hot
There's nothing better than a spot
Of cocoa
Just a cup of cocoa
So come and have a cup of cocoa with me.

Mr Gruber Well, I'll have to get along and get the shop open. And don't forget, left hot, right warm.

Paddington Yes, I'll open the door for you. (*He does*) Good-bye, Mr Gruber, I'll see you soon, I hope.

Mr Gruber Yes, good-bye, Mr Brown.

Mr Gruber exits

Paddington switches on his two washing machines then comes down-stage to the washing and stands between the two piles facing the Audience

Paddington Now, what did Mr Gruber say? Left hot . . . right warm.

Pleased that he has got it right he turns and faces up-stage, then picks up the wrong bundles

The Audience will call out

Paddington puts down the washing, turns and faces the Audience again

Oh, dear. Have I got it wrong?

As the Audience shout out he picks up the bundles, this time the right way round and heads towards the machines. When he reaches the machines he turns round again, puts the bundles down, and very quickly, before the Audience can correct him, puts the washing into the wrong machines

Now, what do I have to do? I know, put in one beaker of soap powder when the machine starts. (*He pours a carton of soap powder into the top of each machine*) That's right. Perhaps I'll have time for my elevenses before the buzzer sounds.

He crosses to the cocoa machine and puts a coin in the slot. There is a whirring noise and some steam comes out, but there is no sign of any cocoa

Oh, dear. It doesn't seem to be working.

He gives the machine a thump and immediately things start to happen. Cups of steaming cocoa emerge one after another. Paddington soon fills the tray and they become mixed with the beakers of soap. He tries to drink some in order to make room, but picks up a soap carton by mistake

Ugh! Soap!

Music

He picks up the tray and is rushing towards the Audience when the buzzer sounds and a red light flashes on the machines. He hurries across and by now thoroughly confused, starts emptying beakers of cocoa into the washing machines. There is a flash and a bang and they begin to froth and rumble like an erupting volcano. Smoke comes out the top. He lifts the lid of one, removes his hat, and tries to blow away the smoke. In doing so his packet of marmalade sandwiches falls into the wash. He leans over and peers into the machine

Mr Curry enters. He crosses and peers into the machine, too

Mr Curry Bear! What's going on, bear? I heard you'd taken my washing and I've come to make sure you're doing it properly.

Paddington jumps out of the way and as he does so something white and doughy hits Mr Curry in the face

Mr Curry Ugh! (*He wipes it off*) What on earth is this?

Paddington I think it's a marmalade sandwich, Mr Curry. I dropped one in by mistake.

Mr Curry A marmalade sandwich? In a washing machine? Whatever next? And what's happened to my washing?

By now the machines have stopped

Paddington It's all right, Mr Curry. I think it's ready now. (*He opens the lid of the first machine*) Here are your socks.

He presents Mr Curry with the smallest pair of socks imaginable. They are now brown in colour

Mr Curry My *socks*? Look at them! They've shrunk. And they've gone a funny cocoa colour! If you've done the same thing to my combinations, bear, I'll . . . I'll . . .

Paddington Oh, I don't think so, Mr Curry. They were in a different machine. (*He opens the door of the second machine*)

Mr Curry Disgraceful! Give them here.

He grabs the ankles of the combinations as Paddington pulls them out. They are now brown and ten times as long as they were before. As he spins across the stage they wrap themselves round him until he looks like an Egyptian mummy

Paddington You see, Mr Curry, I told you they wouldn't have shrunk.

Mr Curry (*helpless in the middle of the stage*) Bear! Are you trying to take me for a ride?

Paddington (*coming up behind him with the wheelbarrow*) Take you for a ride? Certainly, Mr Curry!

Mr Curry falls over backwards into the wheelbarrow and is carried off at high speed by Paddington

Music

The Browns' sitting-room. The family are gathered when Mr Brown comes in

Mr Brown I'm afraid I have some very disappointing news.

Mrs Brown What's that?

Mr Brown Our trip to the seaside is off.

Jonathan Oh, Dad!

Mrs Brown That's a pity.

Mr Brown It can't be helped, I'm afraid. The car has broken down and by the time it comes out of the garage it will be too late.

Judy What a shame. It's such a nice day too, and Paddington was looking forward to it.

Paddington Yes, I've never been to the seaside before.
Mrs Bird Never mind.
Mrs Brown We'll go another day.
Paddington (*sadly*) And I'd got all of my things together too. (*He tries to cheer up*) Perhaps I could put them on all the same and then go round to see Mr Gruber.
Mrs Brown (*trying to brighten things up*) That's a very good idea.

Paddington goes upstairs

Jonathan Poor old Paddington. I know how he feels.
Judy He's been trying on his seaside things for days.
Jonathan I expect he'll enjoy showing them to Mr Gruber. Especially his hat.
Mrs Bird Well, come along everybody. If we're not going out we'd better start thinking about what we're having for lunch.

Music

Paddington approaches Mr Gruber's shop. He is wearing his new straw hat, a large pair of sunglasses, a rubber tyre round his middle and is carrying a bucket and spade. The tyre slips round his feet and trips him up so he decides to wear it round his neck

Paddington I don't know why they call them *sun*glasses, they seem to make everybody dark. (*He approaches Mr Gruber's shop*) Good morning.
Mr Gruber Good morning, sir. Can I get you something?
Paddington Don't you recognize me?
Mr Gruber (*lifting Paddington's sunglasses up*) Why, bless my soul, it's Mr Brown. I thought for a moment that you were a tourist.
Paddington Hello, Mr Gruber. I was going to the seaside for the day but Mr Brown's car has broken down so I thought I would join you for elevenses instead. Is that all right?
Mr Gruber Of course. Delighted to see you, Mr Brown. It must have been a great disappointment for you.
Paddington Yes. (*Bravely*) I expect I shall feel better after a cup of cocoa.
Mr Gruber Perhaps you'd like to sit down in the sunshine here for a while, while I make it. I'll be with you in a minute.

He exits into the shop and returns with a folded deckchair

Here you are, the very thing. (*He hands it to Paddington*)

Mr Gruber exits into the back of the shop

Paddington A deckchair. What a good idea. Just like the seaside. (*He sets it up, sits down but the chair collapses*) That's a funny thing. (*He swings the arm round and pinches his paw*) Ow!

Paddington swings it the other way and gets his head between the two sections of the frame. Everything he does with the chair gets him into a worse mess. Eventually he gets it set up properly

As Paddington is about to sit down a sharp-looking character with an old-fashioned tripod camera enters

Photographer Photograph, sir?
Paddington Where?
Photographer No. Would you like me to take your photograph? Only twenty pence, sir. Results guaranteed. Money back if you're not satisfied.
Paddington Well, it would be nice to have a picture—(*he counts out the money*)—I could send it to Aunt Lucy.
Photographer Won't take a minute, sir. (*He sets up his camera*) Just watch the birdie. (*He disappears under the hood*)

Paddington looks for a bird, can't see one so he goes round behind the photographer and taps him on the shoulder

Photographer (*angry*) How do you expect me to take your picture if you don't stand in front? Now I've wasted a plate—that'll cost you twenty pence.
Paddington Twenty pence! But I haven't even seen the bird yet!
Photographer (*nasty now*) I expect it flew away when it saw your face. Now come on, where's my money?
Paddington You said, "results guaranteed and money back if you're not satisfied . . ."
Photographer And you're not satisfied, I know. Come here. (*He grabs the money from Paddington*)
Paddington That's my whole week's pocket money.
Photographer Hard luck!

Mr Gruber enters, emerging from the depths of his shop

Mr Gruber Now then. What seems to be the matter?
Photographer Oh, here comes trouble, I'm off! (*He runs out and through the Audience*)
Paddington He's taken my pocket money, Mr Gruber.
Photographer (*shouting from a distance*) And you won't get it back!
Mr Gruber After him, Mr Brown, we mustn't let him get away with it.
Paddington Right!

They give chase through the aisles of the theatre. A Policeman enters and joins in the chase but eventually the Photographer disappears and they all return to the shop, exhausted

Mr Gruber Oh, I'm puffed.
Paddington I didn't know you could run so fast, Mr Gruber.

Mr Gruber Nor did I.
Policeman (*taking out his notebook*) Now, sir, what seems to be the trouble?
Mr Gruber This young gentleman was sitting outside my shop——
Paddington —when a photographer——
Mr Gruber —came along——
Paddington —and said he would take my picture. Results guaranteed.
Mr Gruber But he didn't fulfil his promise.
Paddington No. He said there was a bird and there wasn't.
Policeman Hold on, hold on! I've got to get this down in my notebook. (*He licks his pencil*)
Paddington And he took my money and ran away. And that's all.
Policeman I see. Now, sir, your name?
Paddington Paddington.
Policeman No, sir, I said your name, not your address.
Paddington That's right . . . it's Paddington.
Policeman Now look here, young fellow-me-bear, any more of that and I may have to take *you* into custody instead.
Paddington Oooh, I'd like to be taken into custard. It sounds very nice.

The Policeman is about to explode

Mr Gruber Excuse me, constable. That *is* his name. Paddington Brown.
Policeman Hmmm. Why didn't you say so in the first place?

Paddington gives him a hard stare

You say this photographer took your money and then ran off?
Paddington Yes
Policeman Hmm. Well, he seems to have left his camera behind. When he calls at the station to collect it, he'll have a few questions to answer. (*He looks at the camera*) It's quite an old one.
Paddington (*getting under the hood of the camera which is pointing towards the Policeman*) Perhaps there's a bird's nest inside? (*He clicks the shutter. His head gets stuck*)
Policeman I'm a bit of a dab hand at photography myself.
Paddington Help!
Policeman What's that?
Mr Gruber I think young Mr Brown's got his head stuck.

They pull him out

Paddington (*rubbing his head*) Thank you very much.
Policeman Hello! Hello! There's a plate in the camera. I wonder if there's a picture on it? Hang on. (*He takes it out*)
Mr Gruber And there's a developing tank.

The Policeman puts the plate into the small tank on the side of the camera

Policeman Now, we'll soon see.
Paddington What's happening?
Mr Gruber In a few seconds it will be developed and we'll be able to see the picture.

Policeman We may be able to trace him through the person in the picture. It might even be one of his accomplices. (*He pulls out the photograph with a flourish and holds it up for the others to see*) There we are! What did I tell you?
Paddington It's a bit blurred.
Mr Gruber It may be blurred but it's certainly the face of a villain.
Paddington He looks even worse in the photograph.
Mr Gruber What a nasty piece of work.
Policeman Look at those shifty eyes and that weak chin.

Paddington and Mr Gruber look from the picture to the Policeman and back again, comparing the two. They realize their mistake and decide to creep away and exit

It just shows you the sort of person we in the force are up against. (*He takes a closer look at the picture and suddenly realizes his mistake*) Hang on . . . that's not the man we're after . . . that's a picture of me . . .! (*He sits down heavily in the deckchair, which collapses. Struggling to his feet, he looks round, discovers that Paddington and Mr Gruber have gone. He blows his whistle as he hurries after them*) Come back!

Music

The Browns' sitting-room. Mrs Brown is making up a basket of food when Mrs Bird comes in

Mrs Brown If I see another bunch of grapes I shall scream. That's the third this week. Not to mention three pots of jam, two dozen eggs and a jar of calves'-foot jelly.
Mrs Bird I thought Mr Curry was supposed to be ill. He seems to have a very healthy appetite.
Mrs Brown He says he hurt his leg in the launderette the other day. I don't know how long he'll be in hospital.
Mrs Bird If you ask me, Mr Curry will be coming out of hospital when it suits *him* and not a minute before. He knows when he is on to a good thing. Free board and lodging.
Mrs Brown And everybody at his beck and call.
Mrs Bird He has a relapse every time the doctor says he is getting better.

A Postman enters and drops a letter through the front door just as Paddington is coming downstairs, then exits

Paddington It's all right, Mrs Brown, I'll get it. (*He brings the letter to her*)
Mrs Bird I'm certainly not having him staying *here*. So he'd better not get that idea into his head.
Paddington It looks like Mr Curry's writing.
Mrs Brown Yes, I'm afraid you're right. (*She opens the envelope*)

Mrs Bird What does he say?

Mrs Brown (*reading*) "Dear Mrs Brown, my leg is still troubling me although the incompetent doctors say that there is nothing wrong . . ."

Mrs Bird I'm sure they're right.

Mrs Brown (*reading*) "Will you please send some more apples—I didn't like the last lot. They were too sour—and another cherry cake. By the way, two cherries were missing from the one you sent last week . . ."

Paddington (*guiltily*) Perhaps they were loose, Mrs Brown?

Mrs Bird (*with meaning*) Perhaps.

Mrs Brown (*reading*) "I would like them as soon as possible." Do you mind taking this parcel to him, Paddington?

Paddington (*cheerfully*) No. I've never been to a hospital before. I wonder if it's like the "Daredevil Doctor" series on television? (*He puts his duffle coat on*)

Mrs Bird I shouldn't think so for one moment.

Mrs Brown There now. It's packed. And I've fixed the cherries *firmly* in the cake this time so let's hope they don't fall out.

Mrs Bird Explain to Mr Curry that we can't come tonight because we're going out. There's no need to stay long.

Paddington (*looking at his case which stands next to Mr Curry's basket*) Is that my elevenses, Mrs Brown?

Mrs Brown Yes. I've packed you some sandwiches and a thermos flask of cocoa. Drink it carefully, it's very hot.

Paddington (*putting on his hat*) Thank you. I won't be long.

Paddington exits through the front door

Mrs Brown I do hope we're doing the right thing, letting him go by himself.

Mrs Bird I shouldn't worry about that bear. He knows how to look after number one.

Mrs Brown It wasn't Paddington I was thinking of, it's the hospital . . .

Music

A small room in the hospital. A Nurse sits at the desk with a telephone. She is finishing a conversation

Nurse Yes, Sir Archibald. Very good, Sir Archibald.

She replaces the phone as Paddington knocks at the door

Come in.

Paddington enters

Paddington Good morning.

Nurse Good morning. Can I help you?

Paddington I don't know really. I'd like to see Mr Curry.

Nurse (*looking through a list of patients*) Mr Curry . . . Have you any idea what he does?

Paddington He grumbles, mostly.

Nurse That doesn't help. We've a lot of patients like that. If you'll just wait here for a moment, I'll make enquiries at the office.

Paddington Thank you very much.

The Nurse exits

(*Looking round the room*) I don't think this is like the Daredevil Doctor, after all. Nothing seems to be happening. (*He looks at the clock*) Perhaps I'll have my elevenses. I'm glad Mrs Brown remembered to give me some cocoa. (*He fills the thermos cup and takes a mouthful*) Ow! (*He hops round the room in agony*) Ooh! (*He picks up a doctor's bag from the corner of the room, opens it and examines his tongue in a mirror*) I think I've blistered my tongue. (*He becomes interested in the contents of the bag*) What's this? (*He puts on a stethoscope and listens to his own heart. There is a loud effect of knocking,* OFF) Come in. (*Paddington turns and goes to the door, opens it and there is no-one there. Listens to his heart again. The effect is repeated*) Oh! It must be me. I wonder what it's like being a doctor?

He slips on a white gown and skull-cap, clips an inspection-lamp on to his head and hangs the stethoscope round his neck

(*Speaking as a television surgeon*) Nurse! Instruments ready? All right, bring in the patient. (*He puts on his operating mask and paces up and down*) Now this is serious . . . very serious indeed . . . We shall have to send for the Daredevil Doctor.

The Nurse enters suddenly

Nurse Sir Archibald is coming!

Paddington Is he?

Nurse And he's in a terrible mood. You know he doesn't like students who aren't punctual.

Paddington Student? But I'm not——

Nurse He's here now. I'd make my apologies straight away if I were you.

Sir Archibald enters, storming in

Sir Archibald Ah, there you are.

Paddington Good morning, Sir Archibald.

Sir Archibald Good afternoon's more like it. (*Staring at Paddington's uniform*) It's ward rounds today, not operations. You'll be frightening the patients out of their wits. But now you *are* here, perhaps you can give us the benefit of your advice. I'd like to have your diagnosis.

Paddington My diagnosis! (*He begins to unload his basket*) There's a cherry cake, some eggs and some calves'-foot jelly, but I don't think Mrs Brown packed a diagnosis.

Sir Archibald Calves'-foot jelly. Did you say *calves'-foot jelly*?

Paddington Yes. Grant Dexter says it's very good if you're ill.

Sir Archibald Grant Dexter! And who might he be?

Paddington You don't know Grant Dexter, Sir Archibald! He's in the "Daredevil Doctor" every Monday. He's good at curing people. All his patients get better.

Sir Archibald Are you suggesting mine don't? As a doctor, you're a disgrace to your profession!

Paddington A doctor? I'm not a doctor. (*He pulls off his mask*) I'm a bear. I've come to visit Mr Curry.

Sir Archibald (*on the point of exploding*) Curry? Did you say Curry?

Paddington That's right.

Sir Archibald Are you a friend of his?

Paddington Well, he lives next door, but I'm not really a friend. I've brought him some food to be going on with.

Sir Archibald Food! That's the last thing he needs. It will only encourage him to stay longer. That man's entirely without scruples.

Paddington Mr Curry's without scruples! I thought he'd only hurt his leg.

Sir Archibald (*taking a deep breath*) Scruples, bear, are things that stop some people taking advantage of others.

Paddington Oh, I see. I don't think Mr Curry's got any of those, Sir Archibald, Mrs Bird's always grumbling because he takes advantage of others.

Sir Archibald I see. (*Thoughtfully*) Are you any good at tricks, bear?

Paddington Oh, yes, Sir Archibald. Bears are very good at tricks.

Sir Archibald I thought you might be. Nurse, I have a feeling that this is one of those occasions when we don't stick to the book. We'll make the medicine fit the patient. Will you wheel Mr Curry in here, we'll see him privately.

The Nurse exits

Sir Archibald turns to Paddington

I think it's time we gave Mr Curry a surprise—and I think you're the best one to give it. Now, if you'll just replace your mask, bear . . .

Paddington Yes, Sir Archibald. (*He puts on the mask*)

Sir Archibald I'll give you a chance to see what it's like to be—what did you say his name was?

Paddington Grant Dexter. The Daredevil Doctor.

Sir Archibald Now I've had an idea. (*He goes to the door and returns with a tool box*) The workmen left these when they were doing some repairs. When I tell you to get your instruments ready, this is the box I want you to get them from.

Paddington Right, Sir Archibald.

Mr Curry arrives on a trolley—or a wheelchair—pushed by the Nurse

Sir Archibald Good morning, Mr Curry.

Mr Curry (*overdoing the agony*) Ooooooh!
Sir Archibald How's the patient today?
Mr Curry Worse, much worse.
Sir Archibald (*cheerfully*) I thought you might be, that's why we have decided to operate.
Mr Curry (*sitting up quickly*) Operate? Did you say operate?
Sir Archibald Yes, that's right. No good playing around with these things. I'd like to introduce you to . . . a colleague from overseas. He specializes in legs. (*To Paddington*) Perhaps you'd like to listen to the patient's heart?
Paddington Of course, Sir Archibald. (*He sticks the stethoscope under the bottom of the blanket. Mr Curry is ticklish and starts squirming*)
Sir Archibald Ahem . . . I think I should try the *other* end.

Paddington does as he is told

How's that?
Paddington It's got a very strong beat, Sir Archibald. (*He jumps up and down to the rhythm*) It sounds like the "Pick of the Pops".
Mr Curry "Pick of the Pops!" You've got your stethoscope on my transistor set!
Paddington I'm sorry, Mr Curry. (*In his confusion he reverses the stethoscope and puts the headpiece on Mr Curry. He shouts in the other end*) Are you there?

Mr Curry leaps a mile

Mr Curry Of course I am! (*He turns to Sir Archibald*) Is this . . . this *person* going to be allowed to operate on me? He's not big enough for a start.
Sir Archibald (*blandly*) Oh, don't worry about his size. We'll give him a box to stand on.
Mr Curry A box to stand on!
Sir Archibald Yes, it makes him a bit wobbly but otherwise it's all right.
Mr Curry What!
Sir Archibald (*turning to Paddington with a wink*) Now, if you would just like to get your instruments ready.
Paddington Certainly, Sir Archibald. (*He opens the carpenter's tool box*) One hammer . . . (*He puts it on the desk*)
Mr Curry A hammer!
Paddington One chisel. (*He puts it next to the hammer*)
Mr Curry A chisel!
Paddington And one saw. (*He brings out a large carpenter's saw*)
Mr Curry A saw!
Paddington Anaesthetic, Nurse.

The Nurse hands him an enormous mallet

Mr Curry I'm off. (*He leaps out of bed*)
Sir Archibald Ah, Mr Curry, my colleague seems to have effected a remarkable cure. You can leave the hospital today.

Mr Curry Leave? I don't know what you're talking about.
Sir Archibald You aren't limping any more.
Mr Curry (*realizing he's been beaten*) Bah!

Mr Curry exits, storming out

Sir Archibald (*after his laughter has subsided*) It seems we have another free bed in the ward after all, Nurse. (*He removes Paddington's mask and shakes his paw warmly*) Congratulations, bear, I've never in all my life seen a patient recover so quickly. Perhaps you would like to keep your stethoscope as a souvenir?
Paddington May I? Oh, thank you very much. I've never had one of these before. I'm glad Mr Curry's better, I don't expect he'll be needing his cherry cake now?
Sir Archibald Cherry cake? Did you say cherry cake?
Paddington Yes, I brought it for him specially. (*He shows the cake to Sir Archibald. The cherries are obviously a great temptation*)
Sir Archibald (*with a twinkle*) Do you like eating the cherries off the top?
Paddington Oh, yes. More than the cake, much more.
Sir Archibald So do I. It does seem a pity to waste them.
Paddington Yes, it does. A great pity.

CHERRY CAKE FOR TEA (SONG)

Paddington I like marmalade for breakfast
Sir Archibald Jam is nicer
Paddington Not for me
Together But one thing in particular we both enjoy
Is cherry cake for tea
Paddington I like cocoa at eleven
Sir Archibald I like coffee
Paddington Not for me
Together But one thing in particular we both enjoy
Is cherry cake for tea
Sir Archibald Do you think we should sample it now?
Paddington Just one cherry will never be missed
Sir Archibald It's a temptation hard to resist
Paddington We must take only one and no more
Sir Archibald When I see a cake with cherries on top of it
I know for certain I could eat the whole lot of it
Paddington I like lollipops and bullseyes;
Sticky toffee
Sir Archibald Not for me
Together But one thing in particular we both adore
Sir Archibald There aren't so many cherries as there were before
Paddington There's one for you and one for me
Sir Archibald And another for you
Paddington And another for me
Together Cherry cake for tea.

They pick the cherries from the top of the cake and start tossing them into the audience as the scene ends

Music

The Browns' sitting-room. Mr Gruber and Paddington are talking together

Mr Gruber So you're all alone today, Mr Brown.
Paddington Yes. Judy and Jonathan have been staying with friends and Mr and Mrs Brown have gone to collect them.
Mr Gruber And you're looking after the house?
Paddington That's right. I thought I would give them a surprise so I'm going to cook a pie for them to eat when they get back.
Mr Gruber That sounds a good idea. Are you sure you can manage?
Paddington Oh, yes. Mrs Brown has some very good cookery books. I thought I would do some odd jobs about the house as well.
Mr Gruber Will you have time for that?
Paddington I think so. I can paint the ceiling in the kitchen while I'm waiting for the pie to cook. Mr Brown is always saying that he's going to paint it but he never seems to get time. Like the tap.
Mr Gruber The tap?
Paddington Yes, it's got a leaky washer. Mrs Bird has mentioned it several times but he always forgets to mend it. I thought I would do that job as well. Then everybody will get a surprise.
Mr Gruber Perhaps you would like me to drop in later in the morning to see how you're getting on?
Paddington That's a good idea, Mr Gruber. We could have elevenses together.
Mr Gruber Thank you, Mr Brown, I'll look forward to it.

Mr Gruber exits through the back door

Paddington moves into the kitchen and starts the household chores. He sweeps the floor, brushing the crumbs under the mat, then takes down a cookery book, a jar of marmalade and a spoon

Paddington (*reading aloud as he absent-mindedly eats the marmalade*) "The World of Pies and Puddings. Take half a pound of freshly cooked carrots . . ." That shouldn't be difficult—I'll use the electric kettle.

He pops a couple of carrots into the electric kettle and switches on

Now, while they're cooking I'll start the ceiling.

He dips a brush into some paint and climbs a small step ladder

That's not a very good idea, I'll have to go up and down the steps every time I want to dip my brush in the paint. (*He reflects*) I know!

He ties a rope on to the bucket of paint, hauls it over a hook in the ceiling and ties the rope to a convenient hat-peg. Then he takes a notice which he has already prepared and hangs it in the hall. "DANGER—BEAR AT WORK." *He goes back to the kitchen and switches on the radio. As he gets to the top of the ladder, the music ends and the disc jockey breaks in*

Disc Jockey And now it's time for our morning cookery spot. Today it's a recipe for pastry.
Paddington (*nearly falling off the ladder*) Pastry!
Disc Jockey Yes, pastry for pies. Are you all ready?
Paddington (*coming down the ladder quickly*) Hold on!

He gets to the table where his basic ingredients are already in position

Disc Jockey Hurry up, we've a lot to get through. Now, take a pound of flour.
Paddington A pound of flour.
Disc Jockey Put it into a basin.
Paddington Put it into a basin. (*He puts it in too quickly and it bursts into a cloud which makes him sneeze*)
Disc Jockey Pour in a pint of water and mix it well—until you have a nice ball of dough.
Paddington A pint of water. (*He pours it in and mixes*). And mix it well.
Disc Jockey Now while you're mixing it, I'll play another record.

The record starts and Paddington places the bowl on a chair behind the table out of view of the audience. Using a substitute bowl with a ready-made ball of dough he kneads it to the rhythm of the music. He soon has a ball of dough about the size of a football

Paddington Cooking isn't as difficult as I thought. I'd better go and get the washer for the tap before the man tells me what to do next. (*He places the ball of dough on the table and goes upstairs to get the washer*)

After a moment Mr Gruber enters through the back door and comes into the kitchen

Mr Gruber (*looking round*) I wonder where he is. (*He listens to the radio for a moment*) I'll never know why young people like that sort of music. Perhaps there's something sweeter on the other station. (*He switches over and listens to a moment of Mantovani*) That's better! Well, perhaps I'm a bit early for Mr Brown. I'll have a little stroll round the garden until eleven.

Mr Gruber exits again through the back door

Announcer That's the end of our music exercise—and now "Keep-fit". Here's Simon Dorian with your exercises for today.

Simon Dorian's cheerful voice comes in

Simon This is a very simple exercise and one that I'm sure you will enjoy. I hope you've got a football handy . . . you have? Good!

Paddington comes downstairs and comes in the kitchen

Paddington The music has stopped. What do we do next, I wonder?
Simon Pick the ball up and hold it above your head.

Paddington follows the instructions

Now bounce in on the floor . . . that's right. Pick it up again—and lift . . . and bounce. Now we'll do that again but quicker. Remember, this time, no pause.
Paddington No paws! (*A bright idea: he places the dough between his knees and jumps in time with the music*) I've never seen Mrs Bird make a pie this way before.

Simon gives other instructions which Paddington obeys. When the fun is exhausted, he completes the session

Simon And stop! Relax . . . that's fine. Good morning.
Paddington Good morning . . . (*Puffed*) I didn't know pastry-making was such hard work. (*He puts the ball of dough on the table*)

Mr Gruber enters through the back door

Mr Gruber Ah, there you are, Mr Brown.
Paddington I'll soon have some cocoa ready, Mr Gruber. I can't really use the kettle until the carrots are cooked.
Mr Gruber (*a bit puzzled*) I see. Thank you, Mr Brown.
Paddington I wonder if you could help me with the washer, Mr Gruber.
Mr Gruber I'll try, certainly.
Paddington If you could just undo the tap . . .
Mr Gruber Very well, Mr Brown. But I hope you know what we're doing.

He unscrews the tap and a stream of water hits him in the eye. He puts his thumb over the tap and it squirts in all directions

Quickly, Mr Brown. Turn off the main stop-cock.
Paddington The main stop-cock?
Mr Gruber (*indicating with his head a tap under the sink*) Yes. It's that one over there.
Paddington Right! (*He turns the tap one way and the stream of water gets stronger*) Is that any better?
Mr Gruber No, Mr Brown. The other way. (*He tries to stem the flow of water with his hat*)
Paddington Right! I mean left! (*He turns the tap the other way and the water stops*)
Mr Gruber That's better.
Paddington I'm very sorry, Mr Gruber. Would you like to dry yourself?
Mr Gruber I think I'd better, Mr Brown. (*He empties his hat*) I'm wet through.
Paddington There's a towel upstairs.

Mr Gruber goes upstairs

Now the water's turned off it should be easy.

He has another go at the tap

Mr Curry bursts in through the back door. He is wearing a dressing-gown and his face is covered in lather

Mr Curry What's going on, bear? You've cut off my water supply.
Paddington It's all right, Mr Curry, I've nearly finished.
Mr Curry It may be all right for you, bear. I've no water for shaving. It keeps coming and going.
Paddington Perhaps you could try turning the stop-cock . . .
Mr Curry Cock? How dare you call me cock!
Paddington (*in alarm*) Oh, I didn't mean you're a cock, Mr Curry. (*He rushes to the stop-cock*) I mean this tap is. And I'm afraid I can't turn it. It's gone all stiff.
Mr Curry (*elbowing Paddington out of the way*) Here, let me try. (*He has a go*) It's no good. Have you got a spanner and a large mallet?
Paddington (*reaching up and feeling in Mr Brown's tool kit*) Yes, here you are, Mr Curry. They were in Mr Brown's tool kit. (*He drops an enormous mallet on Mr Curry's toe*)
Mr Curry OW! Clumsy nincompoop! (*He recovers and grabs the spanner*) Here, give me that. Now, I'll put it on the tap like this . . .
Paddington Yes . . .
Mr Curry Now, I'll pull the spanner as hard as I can and when I nod my head, you hit it.
Paddington When you nod your head, hit it?
Mr Curry Yes.
Paddington (*looking to the Audience for confirmation that he's heard aright*) Are you sure?
Mr Curry Of course I'm sure. Hurry up, I haven't got all day.
Paddington If you say so, Mr Curry.
Mr Curry Right.

He grasps the spanner and nods his head. Paddington hits it with the mallet

(*Jumping up*) Oww! Not my head . . . the spanner! Ooooh!

He totters round and bumps into the ladder. He tries to steady himself by grabbing hold of the rope and tips the bucket of paint over his head. Unable to see, he staggers across the room and trips over the tool box

As Mr Gruber comes downstairs with his head wrapped in a towel, the Brown family return

Mrs Brown Paddington! What on earth's going on?
Paddington (*uncertainly*) Hello, Mrs Brown. (*Lamely*) I was just making a pie.
Mr Brown Making a pie?
Paddington . . . and painting the ceiling . . .

Jonathan Painting the ceiling?
Paddington . . . and mending the tap . . .
All Yes?
Paddington And it all went wrong.
Mr Curry (*scrambling to his feet*) You can say that again!
Paddington Everything!
Mrs Bird (*surveying the scene*) It's a terrible mess and no mistake, but we'll soon get things straight if everyone lends a hand. Jonathan, will you clear up the pastry . . .
Jonathan Yes, Mrs Bird.
Mrs Bird Judy, you can help Mr Curry tidy himself up.
Judy Yes, of course I will. (*She helps Mr Curry to his feet and takes him to the sink*)
Mr Gruber I'll help you, Judy.
Mrs Brown And I'll mop the floor.
Mr Brown I'll put the tools away.
Paddington (*feeling rather left out*) Can I do anything, Mrs Bird?
Mrs Bird No, thank you, Paddington; I think you've done quite enough damage for one day.
Paddington Judy . . .
Judy Shan't be a moment, Paddington. I'll just see to Mr Curry first.
Paddington Jonathan . . .

But Jonathan disappears out of the room with the pastry

Feeling that he is in disgrace, Paddington picks up his suitcase, takes Aunt Lucy's photograph from the sideboard, and while everyone else is busy with the clearing up, he takes a last fond look round the house and then exits through the front door

Jonathan (*entering again*) That's got rid of that!
Mrs Bird It's a great help when everyone lends a hand.
Mrs Brown Are you all right, now, Mr Curry?
Mr Curry No, I'm not all right. I demand an apology from that bear.
Mr Brown I'm sure Paddington didn't mean any harm. He was only trying to help.
Mrs Brown Where is he?

Judy goes upstairs to look

Mrs Bird He was here a moment ago.
Jonathan He wasn't in the garden.
Judy (*from the landing*) He isn't in his room. And his case has gone!
Jonathan (*looking at the sideboard*) Aunt Lucy's picture isn't there, either.
Mrs Brown Where on earth can he have got to?
Judy Perhaps he was upset because all his surprises went wrong?
Mr Brown There's only one thing for it. We must organize a search party.
Mrs Brown But where can we look? We don't even know where to start.
Mrs Bird (*grimly, as she dons her hat and coat*) I do . . . follow me. If you want my opinion, there isn't a moment to lose.

Mrs Bird hurries out of the house followed by the rest of the family

Mr Curry Hey! Hold on! Wait for me! (*He hurries after them*)

Music

The scene changes to Paddington Station. It is set as in the opening, with a trolley-load of luggage and parcels in the foreground. There are loud noises OFF. *There is an announcement over the Tannoy: "The train about to leave from Platform One is the 'Boat-Train Special'." A Guard's whistle sounds. The Browns rush across the stage, but the train is already moving off. A moment later they walk disconsolately back on*

Judy Too late!
Mr Brown We don't *know* he was on it.
Jonathan I bet he was. I bet Mrs Bird was right.
Judy She usually is. Besides, you heard what they said . . .
Jonathan It was the "Boat-Train Special"!
Mrs Brown Goodness knows where he'll end up.

A Porter enters and carries off a sack revealing Paddington to part of the Audience

Mrs Bird (*following on behind*) If only I'd thought of it before.
Judy Can't we ring up the station at the other end?
Mr Brown We can. But knowing Paddington he might get off anywhere.
Mrs Bird Things just won't be the same without that bear.
Mr Brown You can say that again!

The Porter enters again and pushes off the trolley revealing Paddington asleep

They turn to leave. The Audience draw their attention to Paddington

Paddington!
Paddington (*waking up*) Hello, Mr Brown.
The Browns (*chorus*) Paddington!
Judy You didn't go, after all!
Paddington I did. But I missed the train. I made such a mess I thought you wouldn't want me to stay any more, so I thought I'd better go back to Darkest Peru.
Mrs Brown Not want you to stay?
Mrs Bird Of course we want you to stay.
Judy Even Mr Curry wants you to stay. Don't you, Mr Curry?
Mr Curry Well, er . . . Hmmmmmph.
Judy You see!
Mr Gruber I'd have no-one to share my elevenses with, Mr Brown.
Mr Brown Talking of elevenses . . .
Jonathan It's nearly time for twelveses!

Mrs Brown We'd better get back home . . .
Judy How about it?
Paddington Ooooh, yes, please, I'd like that very much indeed. And I shall never, ever try to run away again.

PADDINGTON BEAR (SONG)

Who has a battered old hat and a suitcase?
Do-do-de-do
Who has his own individual stare?
It must be somebody rare
Who is always completely disarming
And really rather charming?
It must be a terribly rare kind of bear.
Who's untidy and gets in a muddle?
Who loves a marmalade sandwich or two
To munch
For his lunch?
Who is sticky and always in trouble?
Who's the lovable bear
With the unusual stare?
It must be Paddington Bear from Peru
The rare bear
From Peru.

the CURTAIN *falls*

FURNITURE AND PROPERTY LIST

The basic setting is the Browns' house, shown as a doll's house might be, with the front removed. The other scenes are played as insets, or to backcloths. The properties listed below are basic requirements only. The rest of the set should be dressed at the discretion of the producer.

ACT I

The Station

On stage: A trolley with several suitcases etc. on it.

Off stage: Refreshment trolley with drinks, urns, cakes and straws on it. **(Trolley Man)**
Luggage **(Judy)**

Personal: Suitcase containing almost empty jar **(Paddington)**

The Browns' House

Downstairs section contains a living room cum kitchen, suitably furnished with stairs at the rear of the stage leading to the upper section of the house. An easel with a half-finished painting is set in one corner. The upstairs section includes a bedroom and a shower (practical). Roller-skates should be set by the front door.

Off stage: Breakfast items to be set after Judy's Lullaby **(Stage Manager)**

Personal: Sticky cake paper, suitcase containing jar, scrapbook, alarm clock and photo of Aunt Lucy **(Paddington)**
Morning Paper **(Mr Brown)**

Mr Gruber's Antique Shop

Shop front with several old articles outside, including an oil painting and several picture frames.

Personal: Suitcase **(Paddington)**
Vacuum flask of cocoa, buns **(Mr Gruber)**

The Browns' House

Set: Condiments on table (mustard, tomato ketchup, etc.)
Large canvas bag

Personal: Bottle of paint remover, handkerchief **(Paddington)**

Mr Grubers' Antique Shop

Set: Old candlestick
Cups of cocoa
Large cardboard box containing conjuror's outfit

The Browns' House

Set: Table laid with party fare, including cake with candles
Aunt Lucy's photo on sideboard

Off stage: Conjuror's table, top hat, cloth, jar of marmalade, hammer **(Paddington)**
Egg **(Mrs Bird)**

Personal: Toy trumpet **(Paddington)**
Watch **(Mr Curry)**

ACT II

The Browns' House

Set: Washing, plastic laundry bags

Off stage: Wheelbarrow **(Paddington)**

Personal: List. Money. Sandwich **(Mrs Bird)**

Launderette

Set: Several washing machines, powder machines, chairs etc.

Mr Gruber's Shop

Off stage: Deckchair

Personal: Tripod, camera **(Photographer)**

The Browns' House

Set: Basket of food
Paddington's case

The Hospital

Set: Desk, chair, telephone
Doctor's bag containing mirror and stethoscope
White gown, cap and inspection lamp

Off stage: Tool box containing tools **(Professor)**

Personal: Suitcase containing thermos of cocoa and sandwiches. Basket of food **(Paddington)**

The Browns' House

Set: Broom, cookery book, electric kettle, carrots
Paint, rope, notice saying "Danger—Bear At Work".
Basic ingredients for pastry-making on table
Substitute bowl of pastry dough on chair
Tool-kit

Station

Set: Sack and trolley loaded with luggage

LIGHTING PLOT

Property fittings required: general light sources

ACT I

Cue 1	**Judy** and **Paddington** go upstairs *Light upper section of house*	(Page 7)
Cue 2	Shower starts *Lights dim on upper section and come up downstairs*	(Page 8)
Cue 3	Noisy bubbling sound *Lights come up on shower*	(Page 9)
Cue 4	**Judy** ends song *Lights dim*	(Page 10)
Cue 5	Almost immediately *Lights come up*	(Page 10)
Cue 6	**Paddington** opens curtains *Sun streams through window*	(Page 10)

ACT II

No cues

EFFECTS PLOT

ACT I

Cue 1	**Paddington** stares at Trolley Man *Audible "stare" effect*	(Page 5)
Cue 2	**All:** ". . . That's all right by me, etc." *Noisy bubbling*	(Page 9)
Cue 3	**Mrs Brown:** ". . . seven pound tin." *Alarm clock rings*	(Page 10)

ACT II

Cue 4	**Paddington** puts coin in cocoa machine *Whirring noise, steam*	(Page 28)
Cue 5	**Paddington** rushes towards Audience *Buzzer sounds*	(Page 28)
Cue 6	**Paddington** empties cocoa into washing machines *Flashes, bangs, froth appears*	(Page 28)
Cue 7	**Paddington** jumps out of Mr Curry's way *Something white and doughy hits Mr Curry*	(Page 29)
Cue 8	**At the Station** *General station atmosphere, announcements, whistles, etc.*	(Page 44)

MADE AND PRINTED IN GREAT BRITAIN BY
LATIMER TREND & COMPANY LTD PLYMOUTH

MADE IN ENGLAND